# Franz Liszt

# THE
# PIANO
# CONCERTI

## *in Full Score*

# Franz Liszt

# THE PIANO CONCERTI

## in Full Score

DOVER PUBLICATIONS, INC., NEW YORK

Published in Canada by General Publishing Company, Ltd.,
30 Lesmill Road, Don Mills, Toronto, Ontario.


This Dover edition, first published in 1986, contains the
unabridged and unaltered text of the two piano concerti from
the volume *I: Für Orchester. 4. Abteilung: Werke für Pianoforte
und Orchester*, edited by B(ernhard) Stavenhagen, 1914, from
the complete works edition, *Franz Liszts Musikalische Werke
herausgegeben von der Franz Liszt-Stiftung*, published by
Breitkopf & Härtel, Leipzig, from 1907 to 1939.

Manufactured in the United States of America
Dover Publications, Inc.
31 East 2nd Street, Mineola, N.Y. 11501

**Library of Congress Cataloging-in-Publication Data**

Liszt, Franz, 1811–1886.
[Concertos, piano, orchestra, no. 1, E♭ major]
The piano concerti in full score.

Reprint. Originally published: Leipzig :
Breitkopf & Härtel, 1914. (Franz Liszts Musikalische Werke ;
1, Für Orchester ; 4. Abt.).
1. Concertos (Piano)—Scores.  I. Liszt, Franz, 1811–1886.
Concertos, piano, orchestra, no. 2, A Major. 1986.
M1010.L77   no. 1     1986    86-753124
ISBN 0-486-25221-3

# CONTENTS

# Erstes Konzert für Pianoforte und Orchester.

### First Concerto for Piano and Orchestra.

### Premier Concerto pour Piano avec accompagnement d'Orchestre.

### Első verseny zongorára és zenekarra.

*) Das Streichquartett soll durchgängig vollständig besetzt bleiben und nicht in Solo und Tutti geteilt werden, ausgenommen an den Stellen, wo dies besonders bezeichnet ist.

*The string quartet is to remain throughout in full strength and is not to be divided into solo and tutti, except in those places where this is specially indicated.*

On fera jouer le quatuor au complet, ne le divisant en solo et tutti que dans les passages où ce procédé est spécialement indiqué.

*A vonósnégyes mindvégig teljes számú legyen, nem pedig solo és tutti-ra osztva, kivéve olyan helyeken, a hol ez külön meg van jelölve.*

1

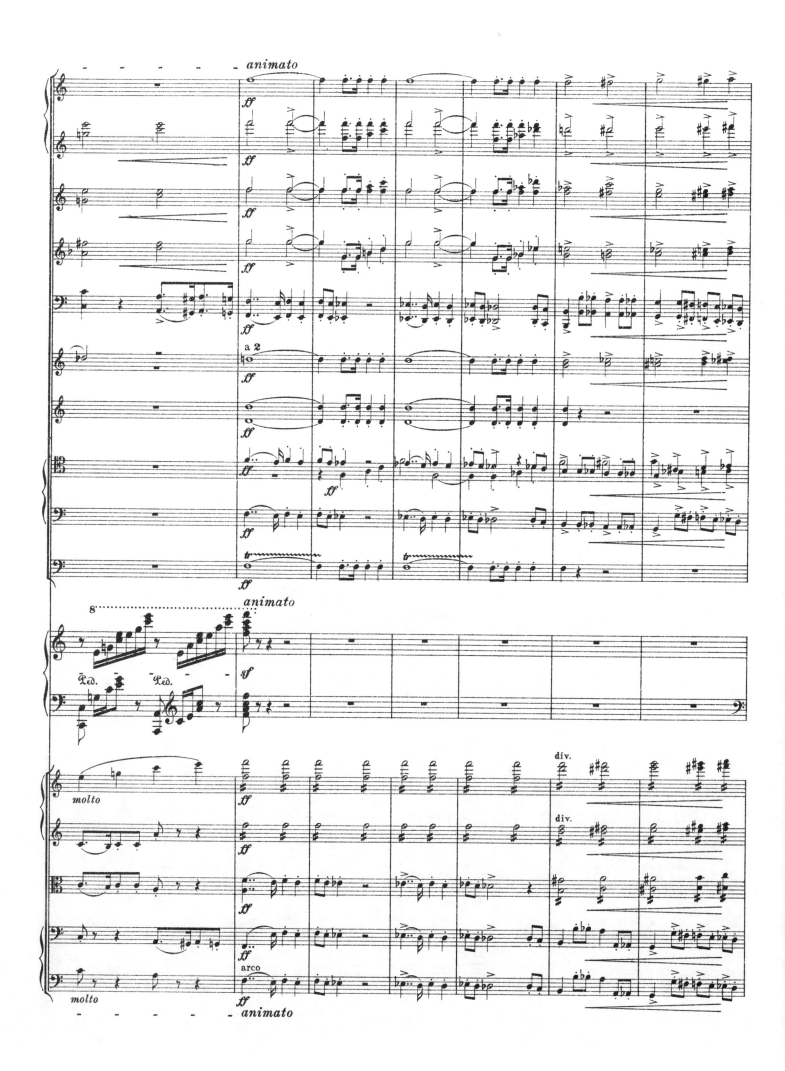

*) Die Tremolos in den Violinen und Bratschen sehr dicht, mit soviel Noten als möglich vibrieren lassen.
*The tremolo in the violins and violas with very close vibrations, of as many notes as possible.*
Les trémolos des violons et des altos seront aussi serrés et aussi vibrants que possible.
*A hegedük és mélyhegedük tremolo-i a lehető legsűrűbbek legyenek.*

*) Der Triangel soll hier nicht plump, sondern fein rhythmisch, mit klingender Präzision angeschlagen werden.
*The triangle is here not to be beaten clumsily, but in a delicately rhythmical manner with resonant precision.*
Prendre garde à ce que le triangle ne soit pas lourd, mais qu'il rythme avec délicatesse et, bien que sonore, soit précis.
*A triangulum ütései ne hangozzanak durván, hanem finoman csengő pontos ritmizálásban.*

**) Wegen Variante siehe Revisionsbericht und Flötenstimme.
*As to Variante see Revisionsbericht and flute part.*
Pour Variante voir Revisionsbericht et partie de flûte.
*A variánst illetőleg lásd a Revisionsbericht-et és a fuvolaszólamot.*

*) Den Rhythmus des ersten Motivs in der Pauke fein und scharf markiert.
   The rhythm of the first theme in the kettledrum finely and sharply accentuated.
   Les timbales marqueront avec autant de précision que de délicatesse le rythme du premier motif.
   Az első motivum ritmusát diszkrét határozottsággal hangsúlyozza az üstdob.

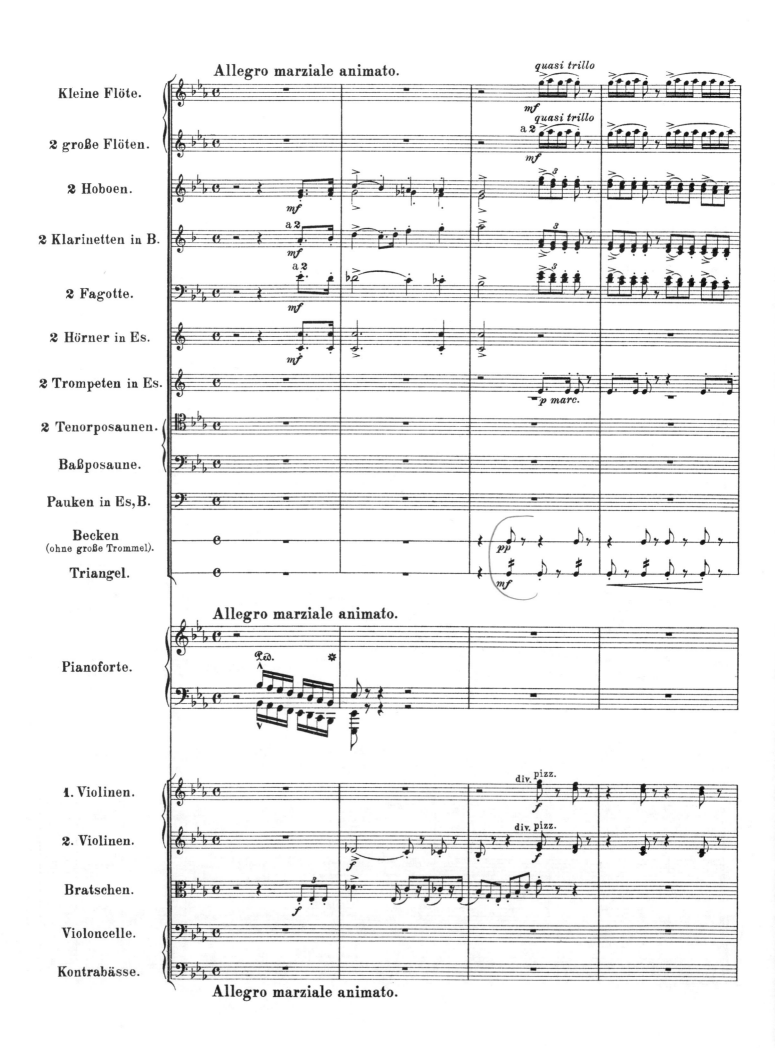

**Alla breve. Più mosso.**

*sempre accelerando sin al fine*

**Alla breve. Più mosso.** *sempre accelerando sin al fine.*

senza ritenuto

# Zweites Konzert für Pianoforte und Orchester.

Second Concerto for Piano
and Orchestra.

Deuxième Concerto pour Piano
avec accompagnement d'Orchestre.

Második verseny zongorára és zenekarra.

68   Second Concerto for Piano and Orchestra

Un poco meno mosso.

tempo rubato

mf appassionato